AF279223

HAL LEONARD
Intermediate
BAND METHOD

BY HAROLD W. RUSCH

For class . . . individual . . . full band instruction.

PUBLISHED FOR

CONDUCTOR SCORE	Bb CORNET & TRUMPET
C FLUTE	FRENCH HORN in F
OBOE	FRENCH HORN in Eb
Bb CLARINET	Eb MELLOPHONE (ALTO)
Eb ALTO CLARINET	TROMBONE
Bb BASS CLARINET	BARITONE T.C.
BASSOON	BARITONE B.C.
Eb ALTO SAXOPHONE	BBb BASS (TUBA)
Bb TENOR SAXOPHONE	Eb BASS (TUBA)
Eb BARITONE SAXOPHONE	DRUMS

7777 W. BLUEMOUND RD. P.O. BOX 13819 MILWAUKEE, WI 53213

FINGERING CHART
for
Flute and Piccolo

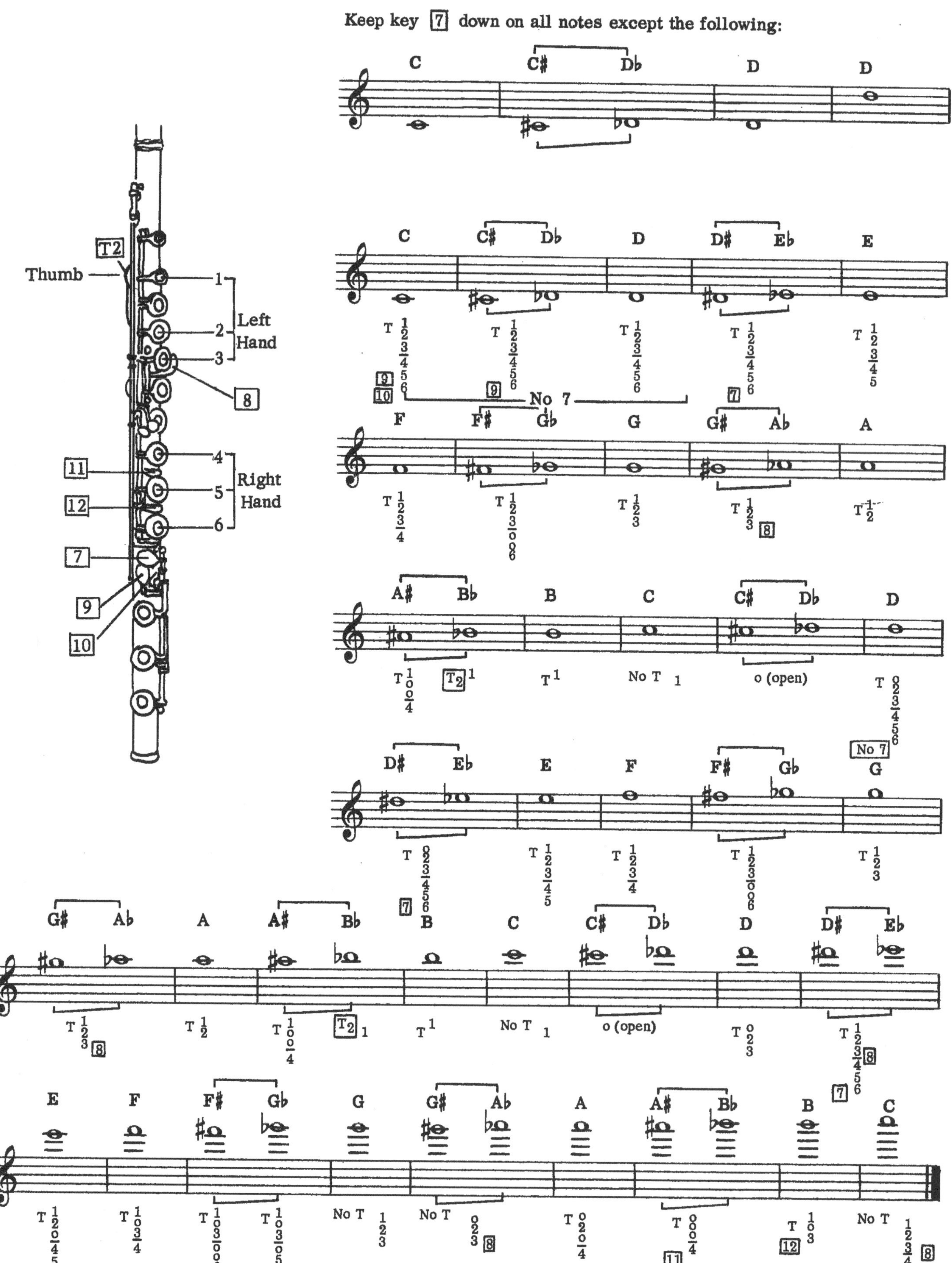

High Register

Studies

Lightly Row

Folk Song

Lightly Row
Folk Song
8
mf

Harmony
Chord Progressions
Play A with B C and D rhythms.
A
9
mf-p
B
C
D

Chorale
Exalted Lord
Andante
Palestrina
10
f
5
p
9
13
f
p

Scale And Intervals
Bb Major Scale
11

Divide each measure into (A) Half notes.   (B) Quarter notes.
Studies
12

13

Intervals
14

Flute

Second Symphony

Haydn

Melody

German

Harmony
Chord Progressions

Harmony And Rhythm

Chorale
Behold Our Faith Divine

Praetorius

Scale
Bb Major - New Register

Scale
Eb Major
30
Ab
T 1
2
3
8
Technical Studies
31
32
Staccato And Legato
33
34
35
Folk Song
Traditional
36
mf
f
mf
Melody
Beriot
(adapted)
37
f
mf cresc.
f
Check the fingering.
Flute

Eighth Notes

38 An eighth note - ♪ - is equal to half of the value of a quarter note - ♩. To simplify reading, whenever two or more eighth notes are written together, the stems are connected by a solid line - ♫ or ♬

An eighth rest - ᛉ - is equal to the value of an eighth note.

The lower line contains the number of eighth notes equal in value to the note in the upper line.

The Rhythm Of Eighth Notes

39 The basis of any rhythm is the "Beat." This in turn must be felt as having Two movements, the DOWN ↓ and the UP ↗. Associate these two movements with the words Sun - Day and Mon - Day. The downward motion coming on the first syllable Sun - ↓, the upward motion on the second - Day ↗.

After a feeling for the meter has been established, divide the "Beat" into "1 and"-"2 and".

When learning to play eighth notes, tap the foot in this down and up motion, which is indicated by the arrows ↓ ↗.

The downward motion comes on the number ↓. The upward motion on the word "and" ↗.

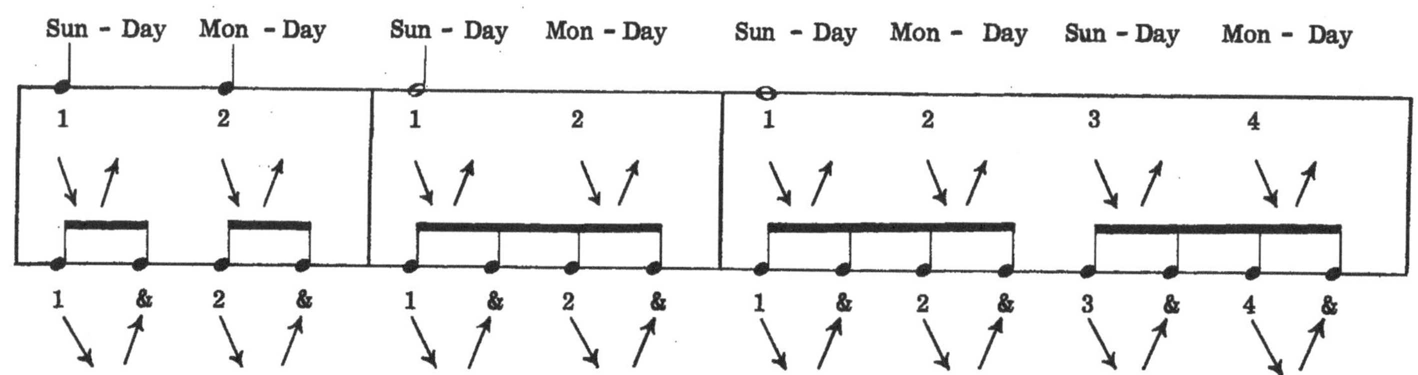

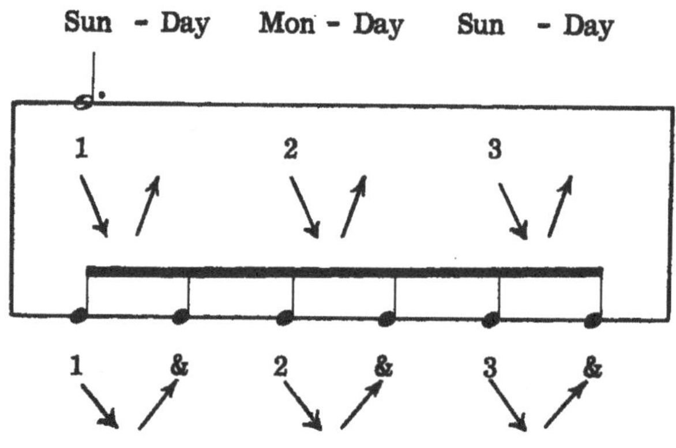

Eighth Note Rhythm Chart

40 (A) Chorale read – Tap foot. (B) Count and clap – Tap foot. (C) Play – Tap foot.
Repeat each rhythm many times.

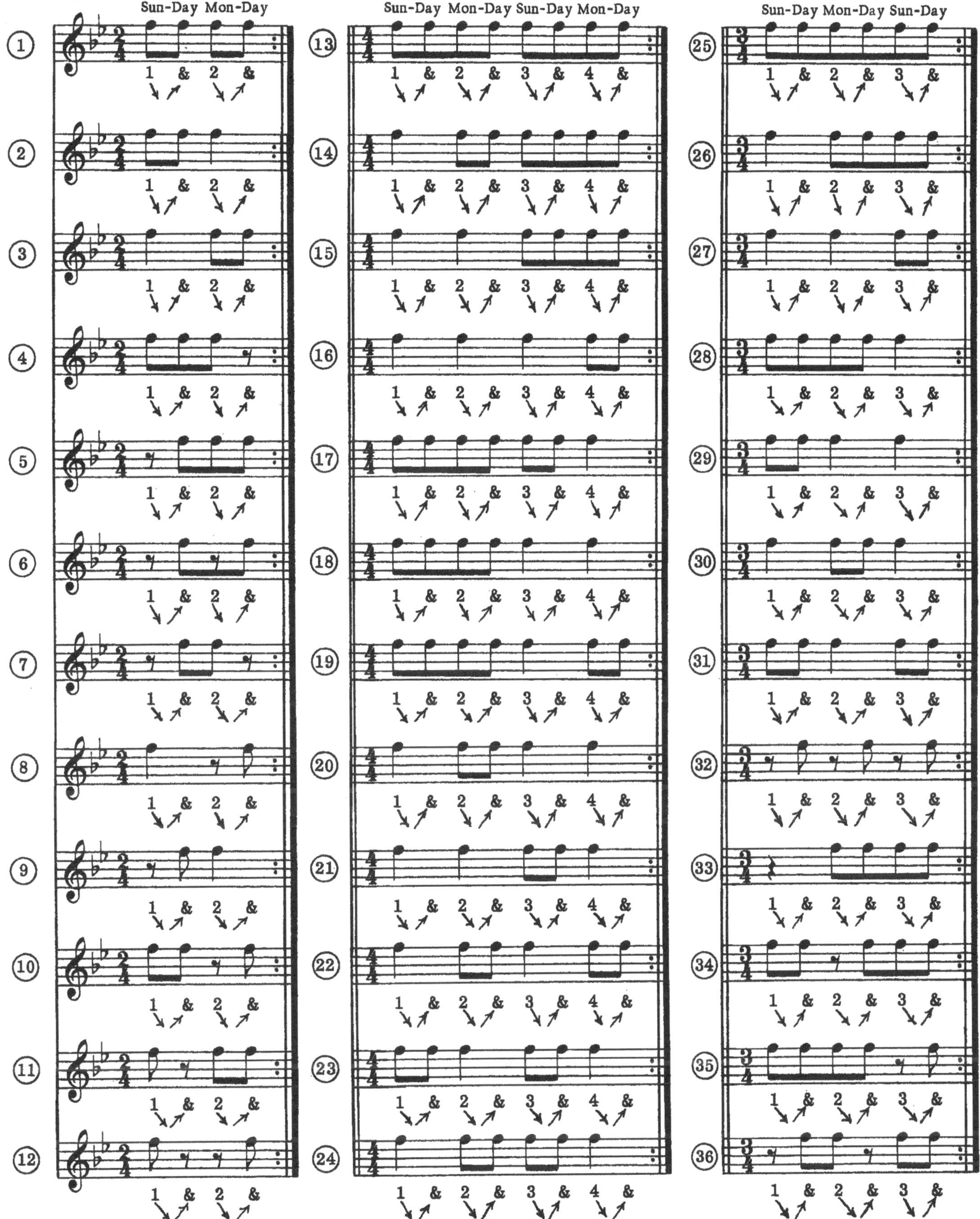

A Rest may be substituted for any note. The counting remains the same.
All or part of each section may be played together.

Flute

Eighth Notes In 2/4 Time
On The 1st And 2nd Beats
(A) Write the counts under the notes.   (B) Play.

On The 1st Beat
(A) Write the counts under the notes.   (B) Play.

On The 2nd Beat
(A) Write the counts under the notes.   (B) Play.

Studies
(A) Write the counts under the notes.   (B) Play.

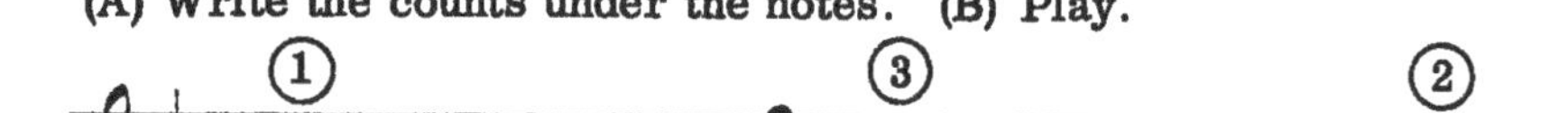

Fox And Goose

Folk Song

✱ Refer to corresponding number in the Rhythm Chart.
✱✱ Check the fingering.

Flute

Rhythm Tricks
Upidee

(A) Write the counts under the notes and rests.   **(B)** Play.

College Song
(adapted)

Good Night Ladies

(A) Write the counts under the notes and rests.   **(B)** Play.

College Song
(adapted)

Eighth Notes In 4/4 Time

One measure of $\frac{4}{4}$ time equals two measures of $\frac{2}{4}$ time.

Studies

(A) Write the counts under the notes.   **(B)** Play.

Robin And His Merry Men

English
(adapted)

First Duet

Moderato

Shortnin' Bread

Allegretto

Traditional

Flute

Rhythm Tricks
She'll Be Comin' Round The Mountain

Eighth Notes In 3/4 Time
Study

Waltz

Duet

Rhythm Tricks
Buy A Broom

Harmony
Moving Chords

✱ Repeat preceding measure.

Flute

Chorale
Rescue The Perishing

Doane

The Dotted Quarter Note

A dot after a note increases the time value of the note by one half.

Rhythm Chart

66 (A) Chorale read – Tap foot.   (B) Count and clap – Tap foot.   (C) Play – Tap foot.

On The 1st Beat

(A) Write the counts under the notes.   (B) Play.

67

On The 2nd Beat

(A) Write the counts under the notes.   (B) Play.

68

On The 3rd Beat

(A) Write the counts under the notes.   (B) Play.

69

On The 1st And 3rd Beats

(A) Write the counts under the notes.   (B) Play.

70

All Through The Night

Welsh Folk Song

Folk Song

German

In The Gloaming

Harrison

Chime Again

Folk Song

Harmony And Rhythm
Deck The Hall

Welsh Air

Moderato

America

Smith - Carey

Moderato

Scale
Ab Major - New Register

(A) Divide each measure into (A) Half notes.   (B) Quarter notes.

Flute

Two Octave Scale

Technical Studies

Santa Lucia

Italian Folk Song

85 Andantino

Playing Independent Parts
The Bell

Traditional

Moderato

86

Sixteenth Notes

87 A sixteenth note- ♬ -is equal to half the value of an eighth note- ♪ -or one fourth the value of a quarter note- ♩ . Two sixteenth notes equal one eighth note ♪♪=♪, and four sixteenth notes equal one quarter note ♪♪♪♪=♩ . To simplify reading, whenever two or more sixteenth notes are written together, the stems are connected by two solid lines-♬ or ♬♬ .

A sixteenth rest- ♽ -is equal to the value of a sixteenth note, and may be substituted for any one note. The counting remains the same.

The lower staff- C -contains the number of sixteenth notes equal in value to the notes in the upper staves- A or B.

⊕ Check the fingering.
Flute

The Rhythm Of Sixteenth Notes

88 Review the "down" and "up" movements of the "beat". Associate these two movements with the words Jan-U-A-Ry and Feb-Ru-A-Ry.   The downward motion coming on the first two syllables- Jan-U ↓ ; the upward motion on the last two - A-Ry ↗ . After a feeling for the meter has been established, divide the "beat" into 1-e-&-a, 2-e-&-a- etc. The rhythm of the counting corresponds to the rhythm of the words January and February.

When learning to play sixteenth notes, tap the foot in the down and up motion- 1-e-&-a, 2-e-&-a.

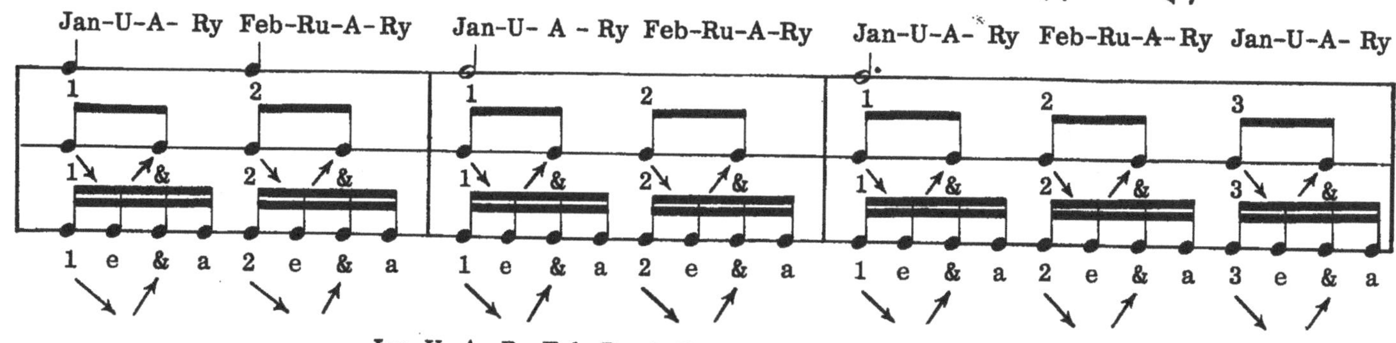

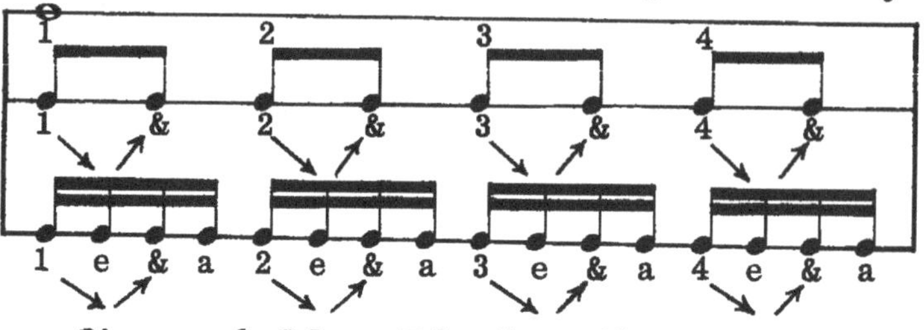

Sixteenth Note Rhythm Chart

89 (A) Chorale read - Tap foot.   (B) Count and clap - Tap foot.   (C) Play - Tap foot.
Repeat each rhythm many times.

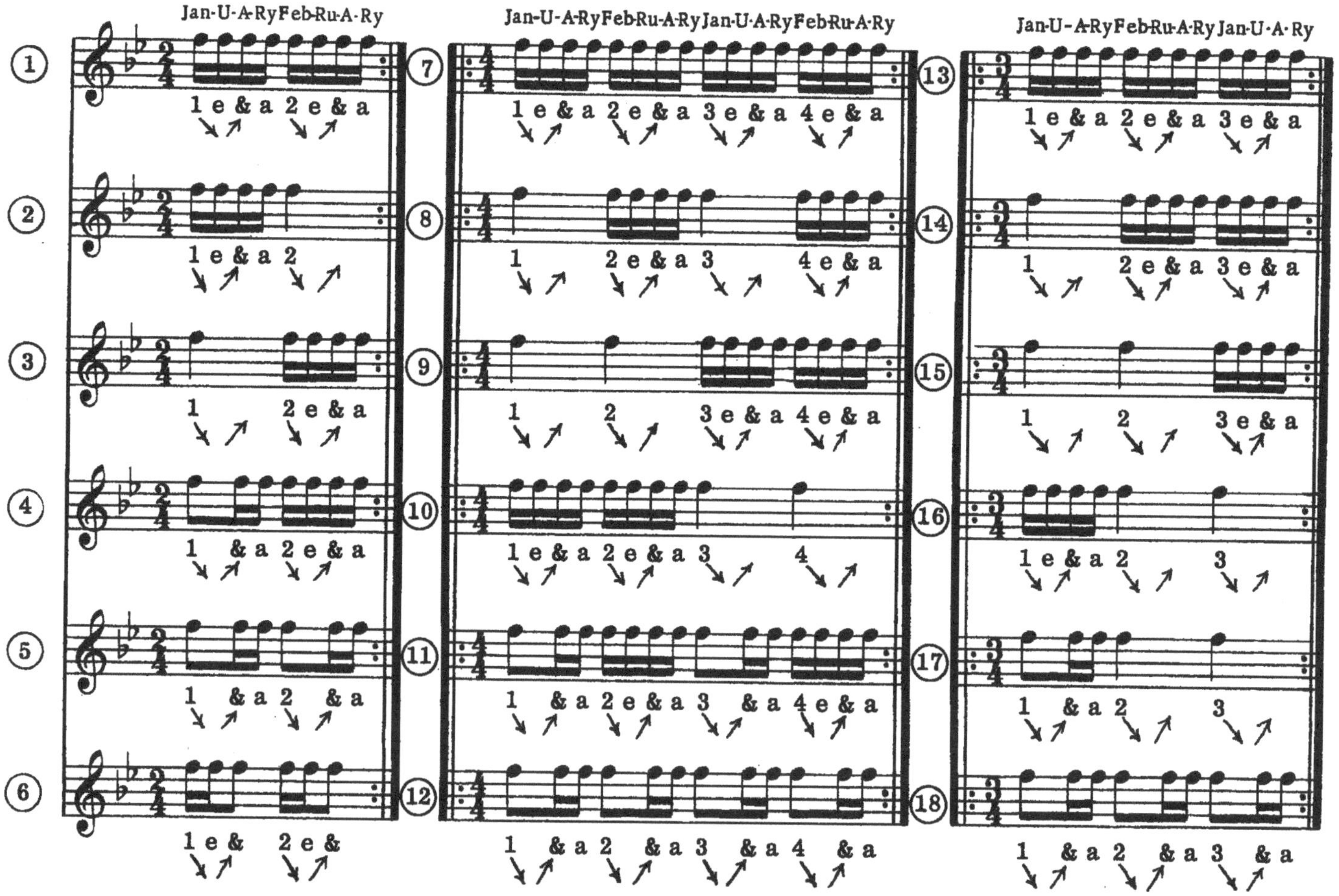

A Rest may be substituted for any note. The counting remains the same.
All or part of each section may be played together.

Sixteenth Notes In 2/4 Time

On The 1st And 2nd Beats

(A) Write the counts under the notes. (B) Play.

On The 1st Beat

(A) Write the counts under the notes. (B) Play.

On The 2nd Beat

(A) Write the counts under the notes. (B) Play.

Study

(A) Write the counts under the notes. (B) Play.

Sixteenth Notes In 4/4 Time

One measure of $\frac{4}{4}$ time equals two measures of $\frac{2}{4}$ time.

Studies

(A) Write the counts under the notes. (B) Play.

Sixteenth Notes In 3/4 Time
Studies

(A) Write the counts under the notes. **(B) Play.**

Sixteenth Notes With Eighth Notes
Studies In 2/4 Time

(A) Write the counts under the notes. **(B) Play.**

Study

(A) Write the counts under the notes. **(B) Play.**

Rakes Of Mallow

Irish Folk Tune

Duet
American Patrol

Meacham

Studies In 4/4 Time

(A) Write the counts under the notes.   **(B)** Play.

Etude

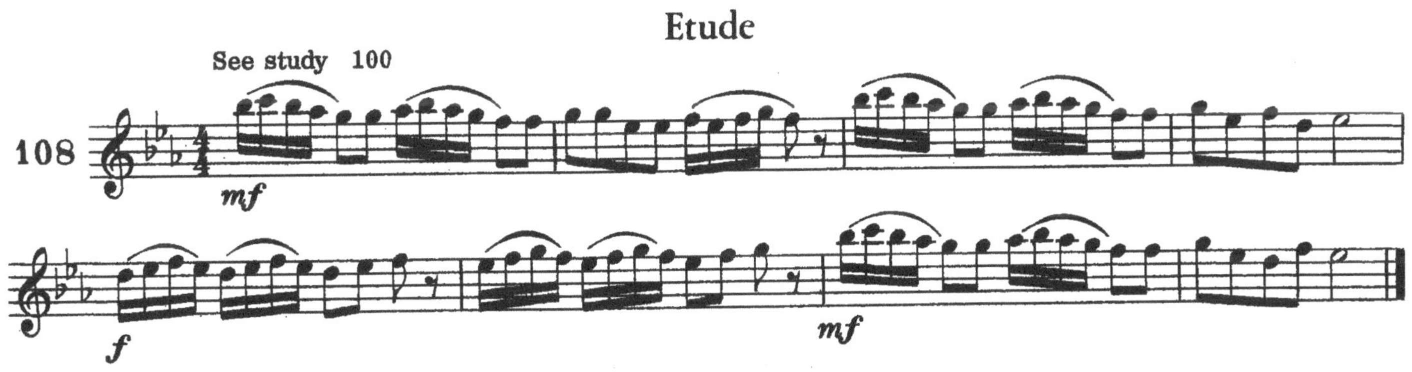

Flute

Scale Studies

(A) Write the counts under the notes.   (B) Play.

Duet
Folk Dance

The Dotted Eighth Note
Rhythm Chart

117 (A) Chorale read – Tap foot. (B) Count and clap – Tap foot. (C) Play – Tap foot.

This rhythm may also be
associated with the words –

Day   to Day   to Day, etc.

Emphasis is placed on "Day".
Count: 1 - a - 2 - a - etc.

Studies

(A) Write the counts under the notes. (B) Play.

Flute

Duet
Battle Hymn Of The Republic

Technical Studies

Long Tones

Scale Study

Pares

132

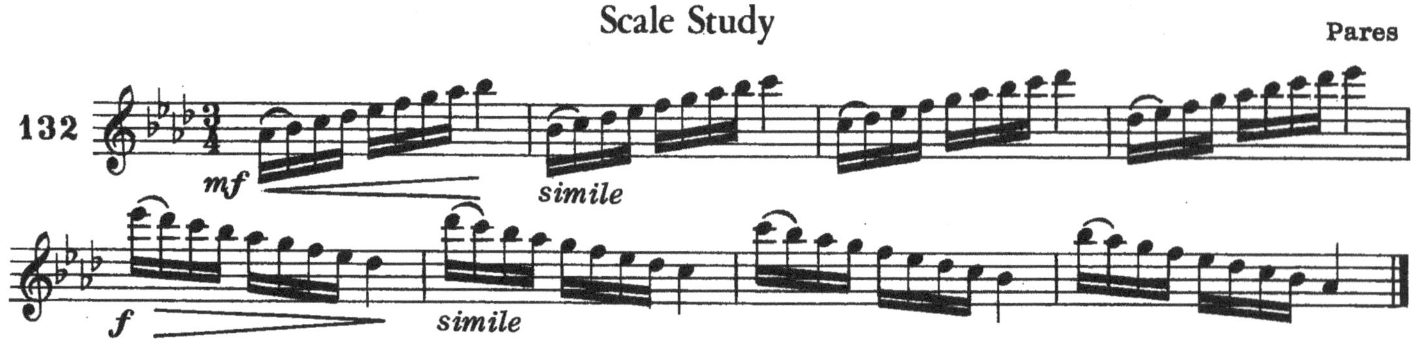

Chromatics

CHROMATIC means ascending or descending by half steps.

ENHARMONIC TONES are notes that sound and finger the same, but are written on different degrees of the staff and have different names.

Enharmonic Tones

133 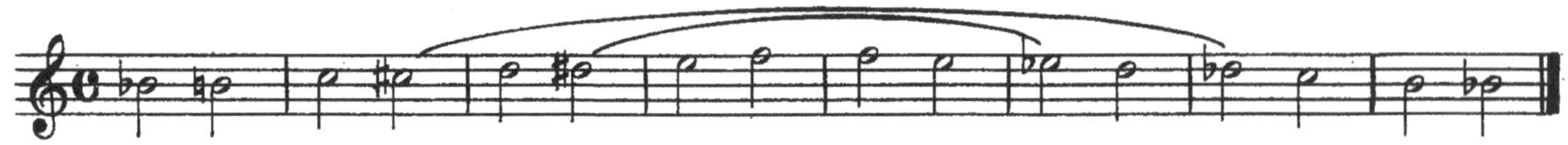

134 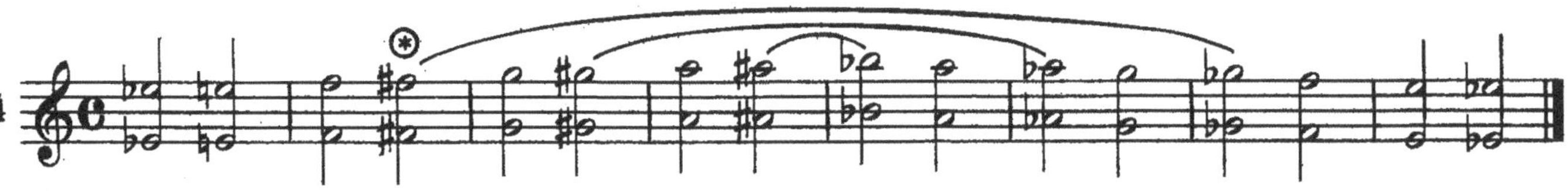

⊛ Check the fingering.

Chromatic Scale

Use correct fingering

135 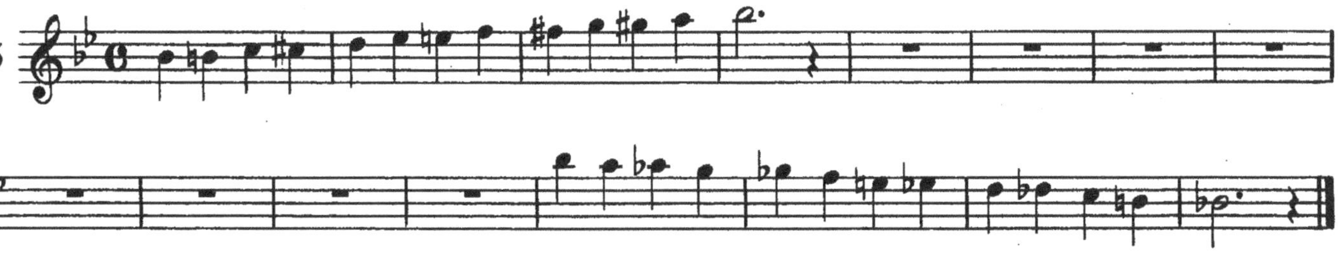

Etude

Czerny (adapted)

136 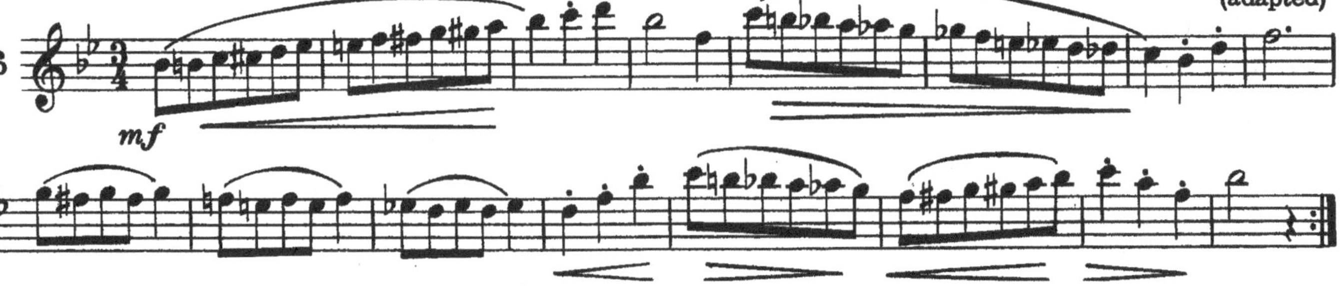

Duet
Flower Of Damascus

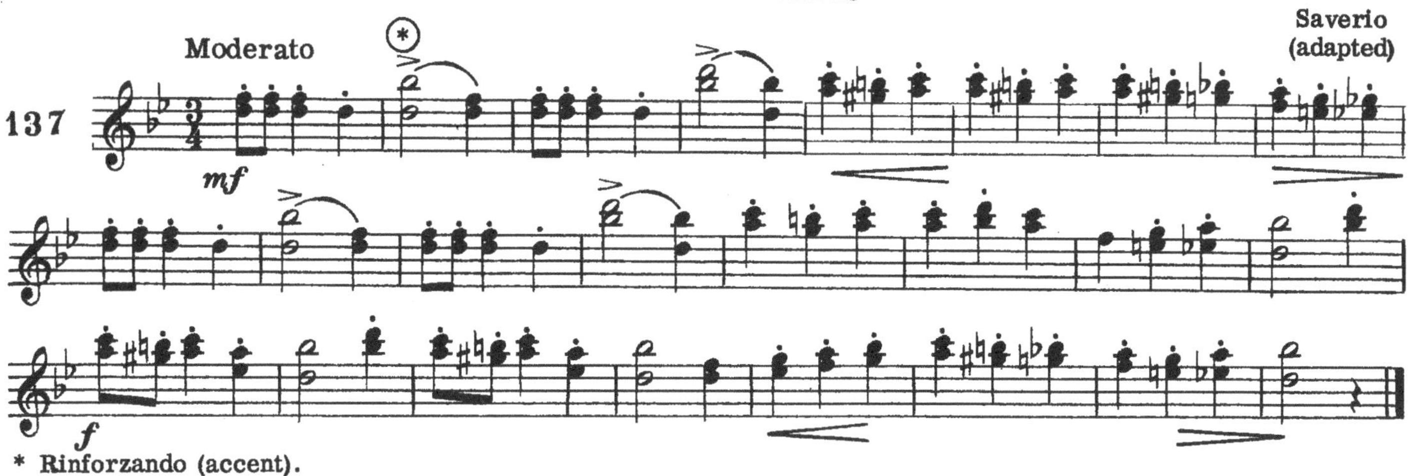

* Rinforzando (accent).

Six - Eight Rhythm

138 In this rhythm, an eighth note is the unit for counting.

$\dfrac{6}{8}$ Six counts in a measure.
An eighth note receives one count.

A quarter note – ♩ – receives two counts; a dotted quarter note – ♩. – three counts; a dotted half note – ♩. – six counts. Sixteenth notes – ♪ or ♫ – will receive one half count each. A rest of like value may be substituted for any note without changing the counting.

When counting this rhythm, emphasize counts ONE and FOUR by tapping the foot on these counts: 1 2 3 4 5 6. Practice will develop a feeling for the rhythm of SIX counts to a measure, but only TWO "Beats". Thus in fast tempo the dotted quarter note – ♩. – becomes the unit of a count and "Beat".

Six - Eight Rhythm Chart

139 (A) Count and clap – Tap foot. (B) Play – Tap foot.
Repeat each rhythm many times.

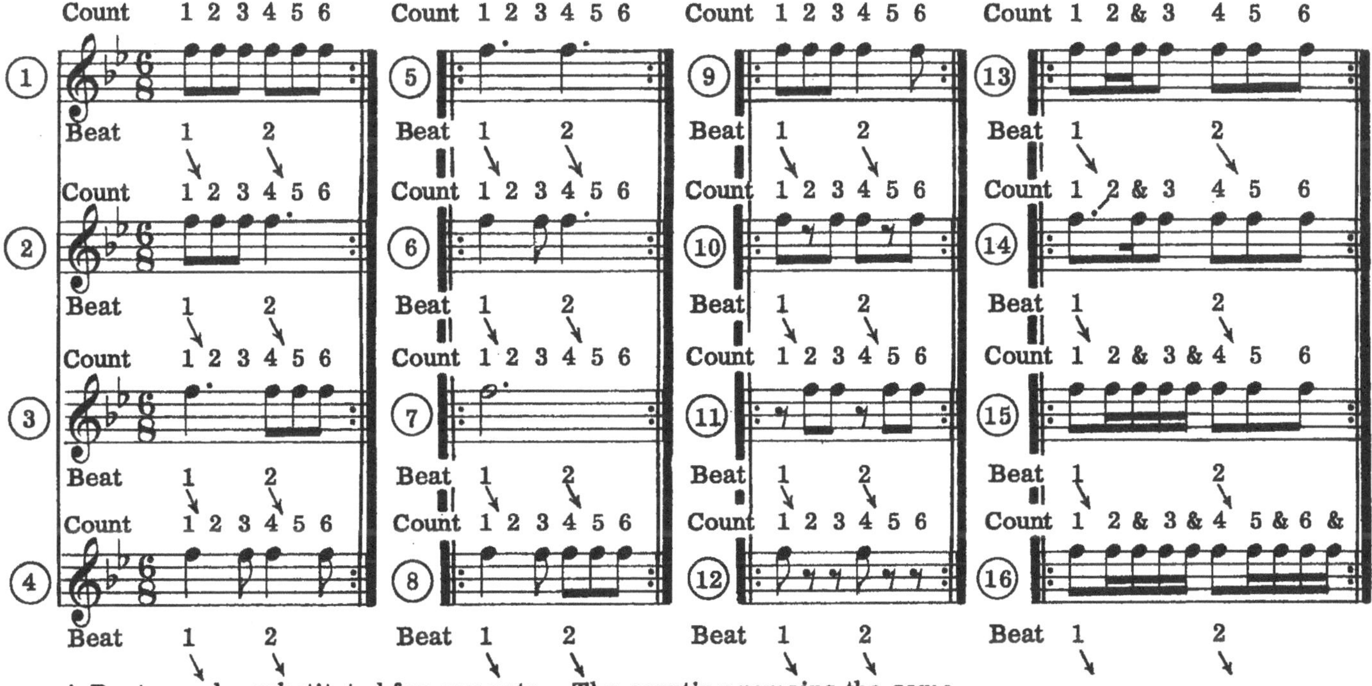

A Rest may be substituted for any note. The counting remains the same.
All or part of each section may be played together.

Practice the following studies counting SIX to a measure. Accent counts ONE and FOUR with a "Beat". Then review all studies counting and beating TWO to a measure. The dotted quarter note (♩.) will become the unit of a count and "Beat".

Six - Eight Time
Studies

(A) Write the counts under the notes.   (B) Play.

Hunters Song

Harmony And Rhythm

Scherzino

Le Couppey

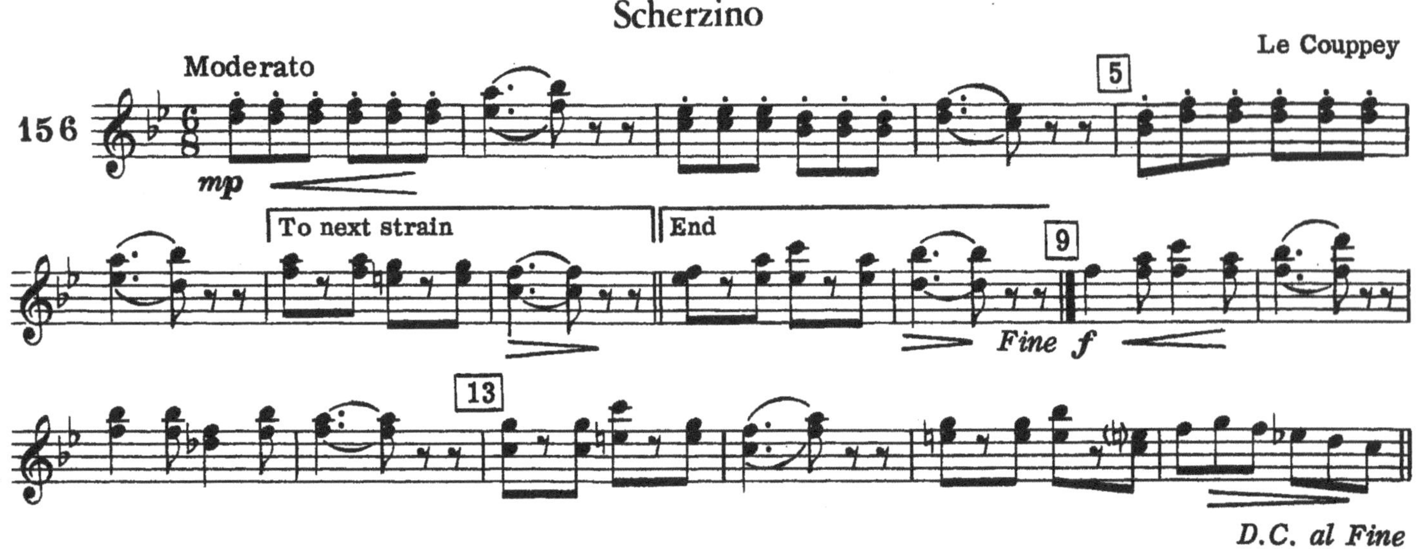

Technical Studies
Chromatic Scale

(A) Check the enharmonic tones. (B) Use correct fingerings.

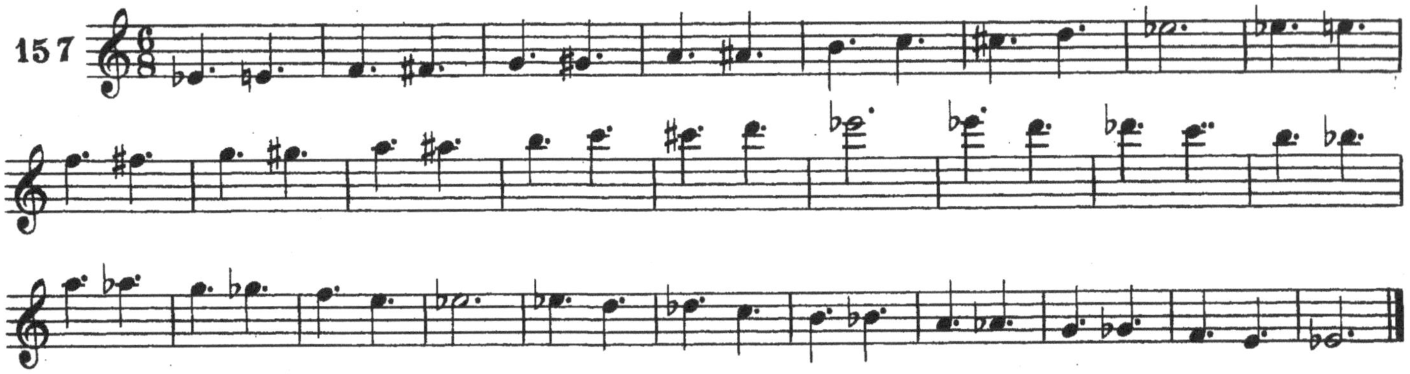

Studies

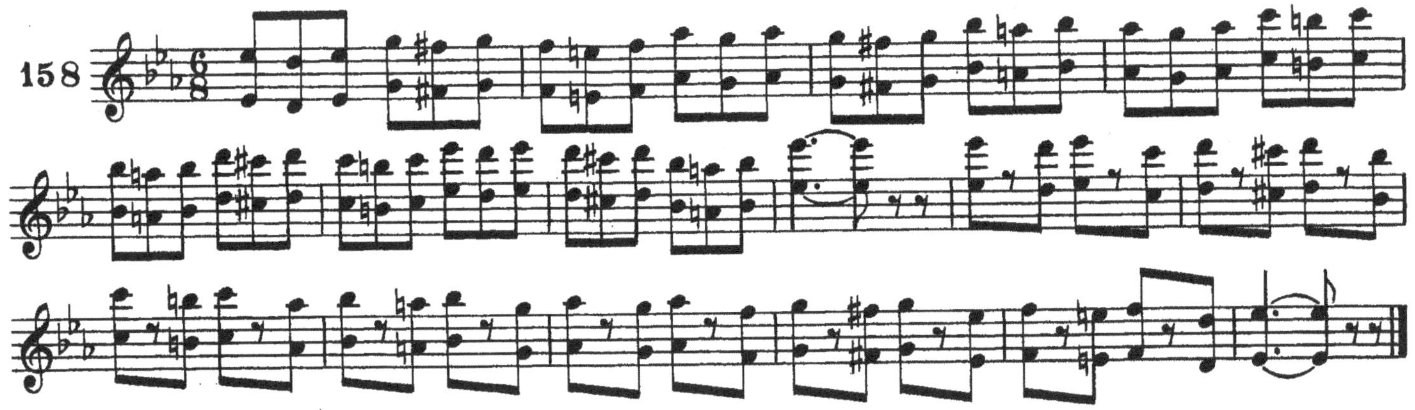

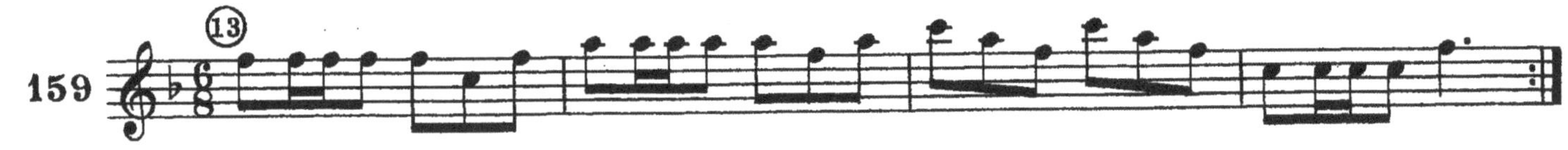

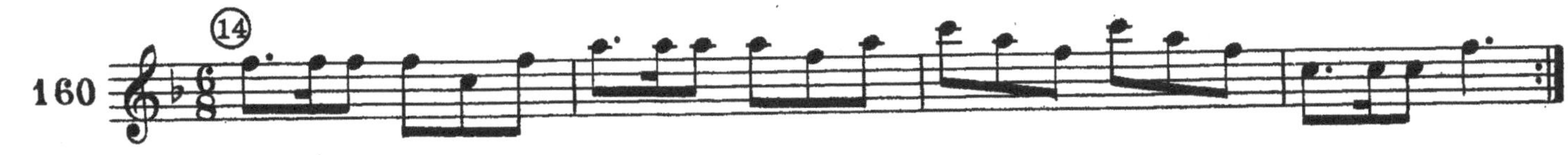

Etude

Triplets

163 TRIPLETS are groups of THREE equal notes played in the time of two notes of the same de-nomination. A triplet of eighth notes - (♪♪♪) is equal in time value to two eighth notes - (♫) or one quarter note (♩).

Triplets are indicated by a number "3" placed over or under a group of notes.

The Rhythm Of Triplets

164 The rhythm of triplets is THREE to the "Beat". Tap the foot in a ONE - \ - TWO - \ - rhythm and associate the word Sa-Tur-Day - Sa-Tur-Day with the "Beats".
Pronounce each syllable distinctly and with equal emphasis: Sa- Tur - Day   Sa - Tur - Day

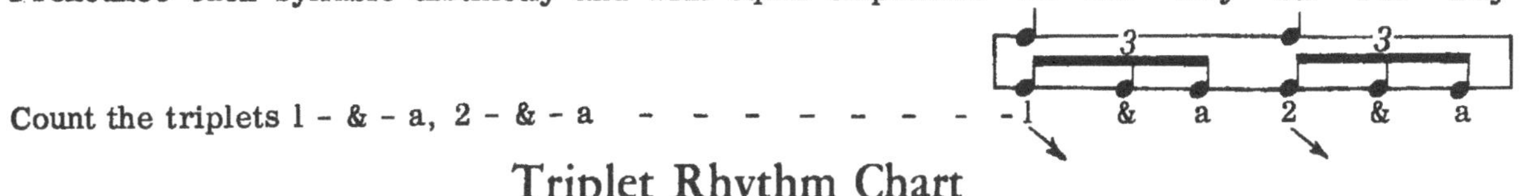

Count the triplets 1 - & - a, 2 - & - a - - - - - - - - -1   &   a   2   &   a

Triplet Rhythm Chart

165 (A) Chorale read - Tap foot.   (B) Count and clap - Tap foot.   (C) Play - Tap foot.
Repeat each rhythm many times.

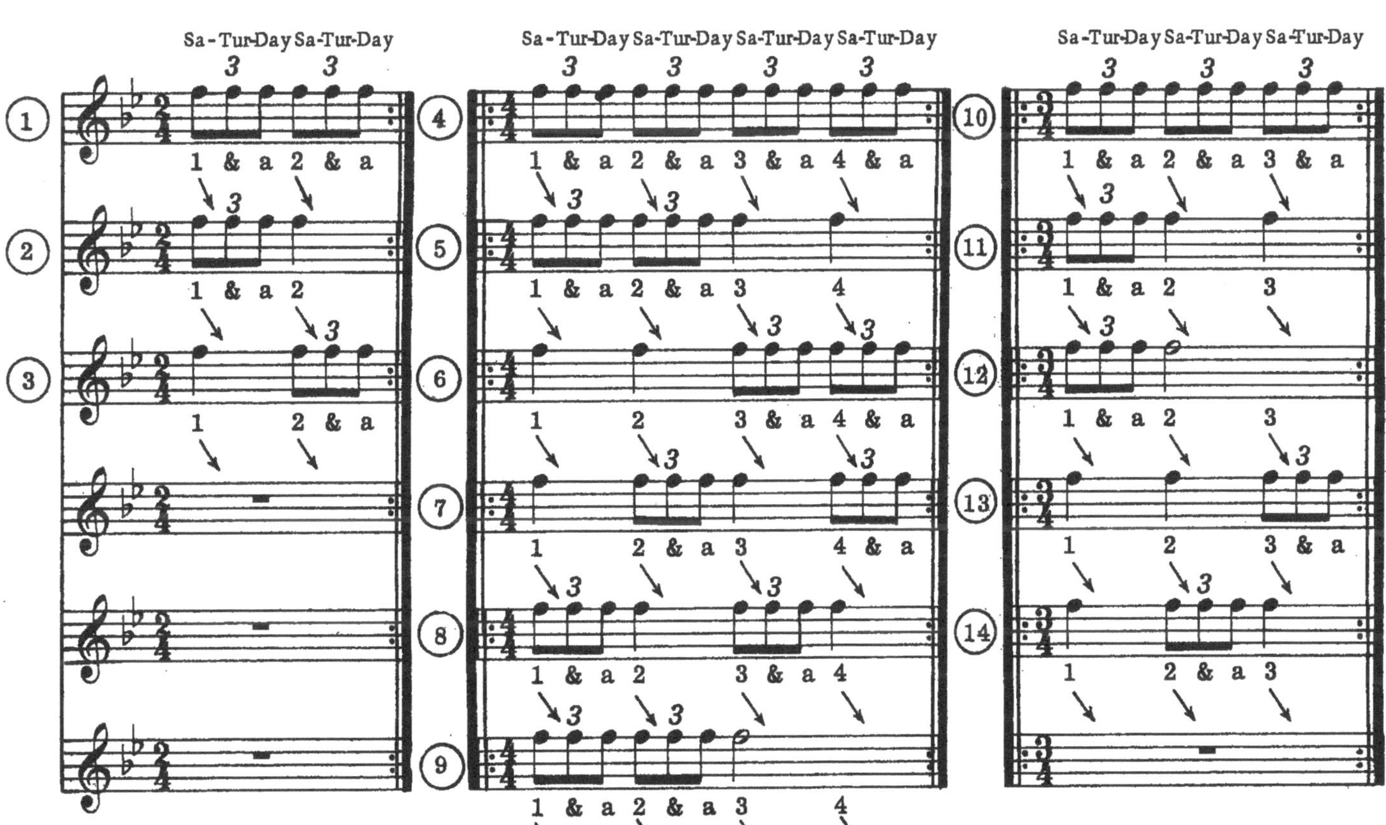

A Rest may be substituted for any note. The counting remains the same.
Flute   All or part of each section may be played together.

Triplets In 2/4 Time
Studies

(A) Write the counts under the notes.   (B) Play.

Triplets In 4/4 Time
Studies

(A) Write the counts under the notes.   (B) Play.

Etude

Czerny
(adapted)

Triplets In 3/4 Time

(A) Write the counts under the notes.   (B) Play.

La Gazza Ladra

Rossini

Flute

Duets

Whistling

Studies

(A) Write the counts under the notes.   (B) Play.

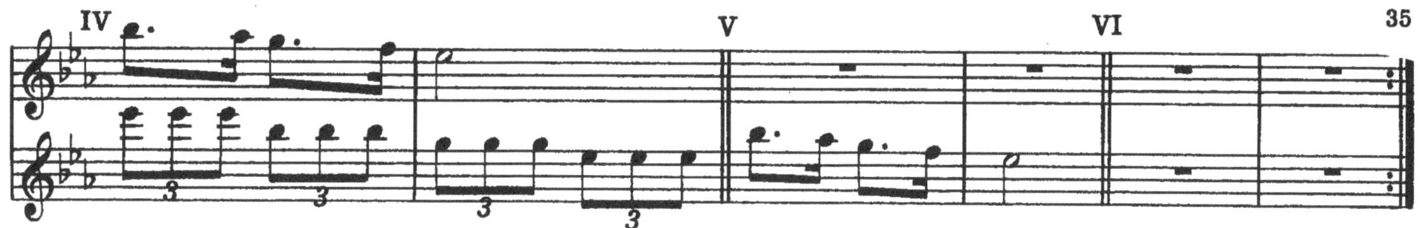

Alla Breve Time

186 Alla Breve - $\frac{2}{2}$ -, or Cut Time - ¢ - is played the same as - $\frac{2}{4}$ - time - TWO "Beats" to a measure. However, each note receives half the value that was given it in $\frac{2}{4}$ or $\frac{4}{4}$ time.

A whole note -(𝅝)- receives two counts, a half note (𝅗𝅥) - one count, a quarter note -(♩)- 1/2 count, and an eighth note (♪) or (♫) - 1/4 count.

187 The following two lines have the same "Beat" and rhythm. Use the word associations previously learned in $\frac{2}{4}$ time.

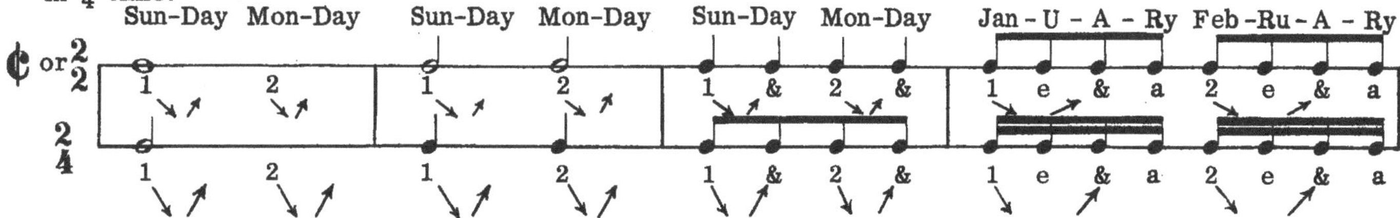

Alla Breve Rhythm Chart

188 (A) Chorale read - Tap foot. (B) Count and clap - Tap foot. (C) Play - Tap foot.
Repeat each rhythm many times.

The rhythm - ♩. ♪ ♩. ♪ may also be associated with the words:

Day to Day to Day, etc.

Count: 1 - a - 2 - a, etc.

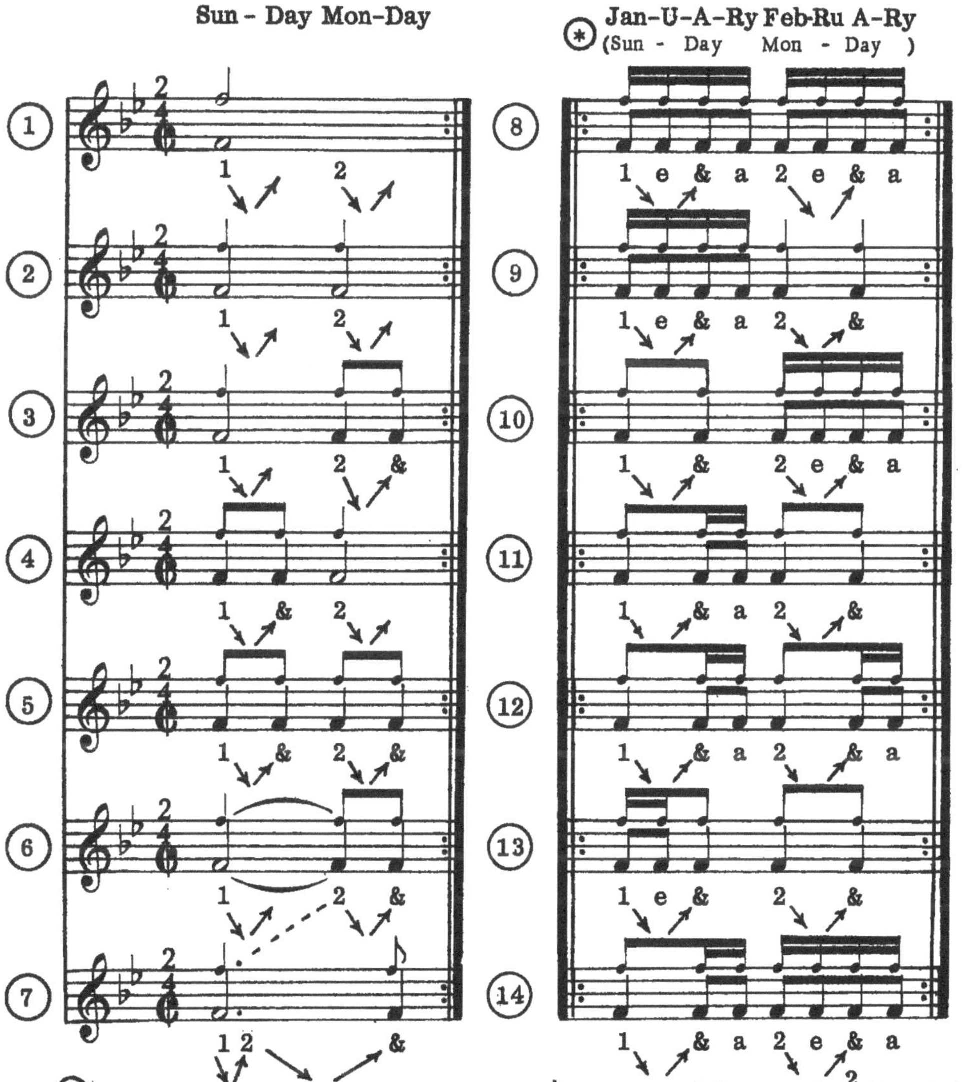

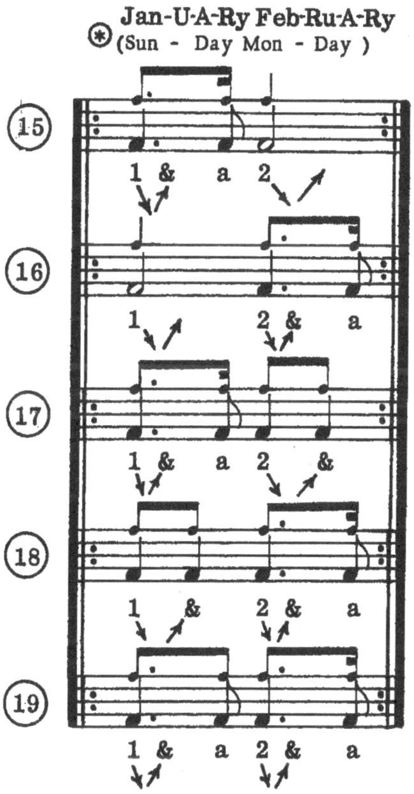

(*) To chorale read the quarter notes in ¢ time. (Eighth notes in $\frac{2}{4}$ time.) A rest may be substituted for any note. The counting remains the same. All or part of each section may be played together.

Studies

(A) Write the counts under the notes.   (B) Play.

Rests In Alla Breve Time
Studies

(A) Write the counts under the notes and rests.   **(B)** Play.

The Dotted Half Note In Alla Breve Time
Study

(A) Write the counts under the notes.   **(B)** Play.

Eighth Notes In AllaBreve Time
Studies

(A) Write the counts under the notes.   **(B)** Play.

Flute

Manhattan Beach March

Duet
She'll Be Comin' Round The Mountain
Folk Song
Allegretto
211
mf
D.C.
Harmony And Rhythm
Blue Bells Of Scotland
Folk Song
Moderato
(unis.)
(divisi)
5
212
mf
9
13
f
mf
Melody And Accompaniment
Stars And Stripes Forever
Sousa
March tempo
5
x
213
mp
y
9
13
17
21
25
29
Flute

214 Syncopation

Syncopation introduces notes on the unaccented "Beat"; or off the "Beat" entirely.
The notes are carried past the next "Beat" where the accent would normally fall.
To better understand a syncopated figure, divide the measure into notes of the
smallest denomination in the measure. Write in the counts and then tie the notes
together that will produce the syncopated rhythm. Refer to the Rhythm Chart.

Syncopation Rhythm Chart

215 (A) Compare the two lines. (B) Count and clap – Tap foot. (C) Play – Tap foot.
Repeat each rhythm many times.

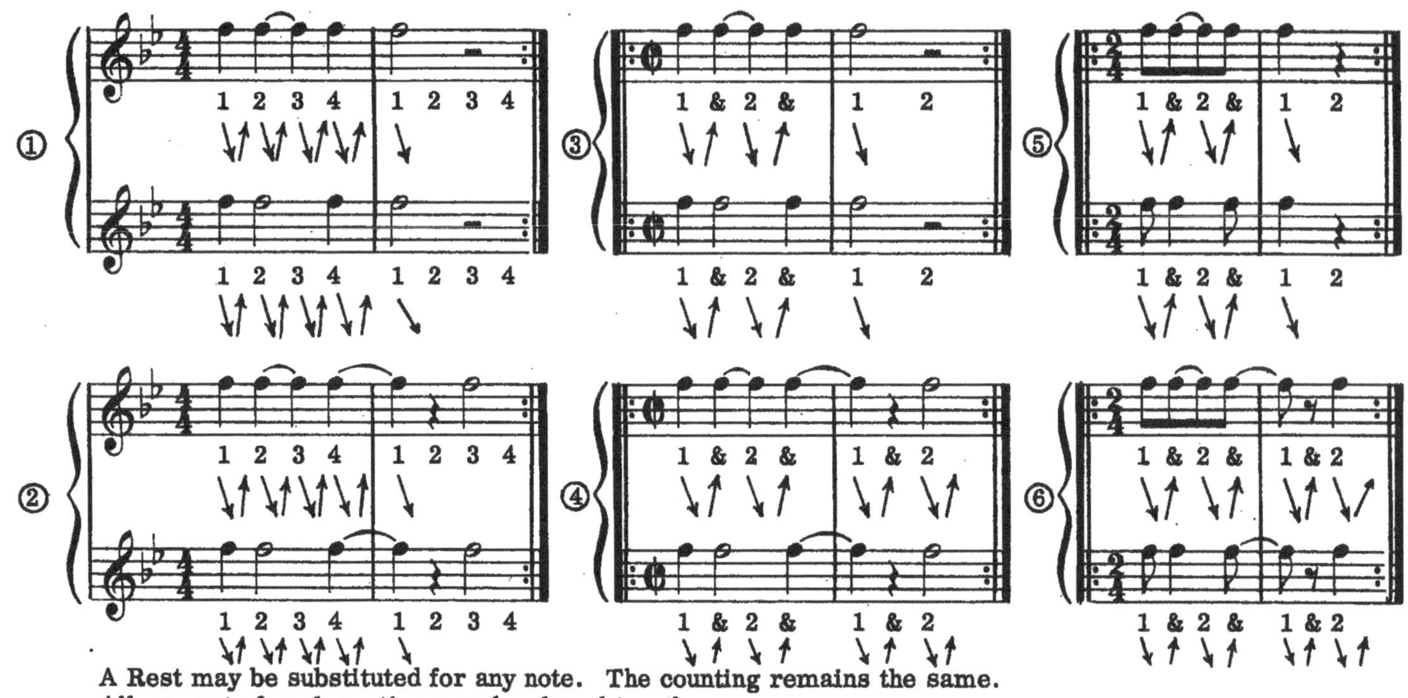

A Rest may be substituted for any note. The counting remains the same.
All or part of each section may be played together.

Syncopation In 4/4 And ¢ Time

Study

(A) Write the counts under the notes and rests. (B) Play.

216

Etude

217

Our Boys Will Shine

Study

(A) Write the counts under the notes.   (B) Play.
224
Dese Bones
Folk Song
(adapted)
225
mp
Duet
The Caissons Go Rolling Along
Gruber
March tempo
226
mf
1.
2.
f
Harmony And Rhythm
L'il Liza Jane
Allegretto
(unis.)
(divisi)
5
Lachau
227
mp
9
13
mf
D.C.
Dance Song
Allegro
5
Czech
228
mf
9
13
17
21
f

Major Scales, Chords And Intervals

⊛ High G.
(A) Devise various articulations.   (B) Use correct fingerings, including auxiliary.

Flute

Db Major

X Scale
Y Chords
241
Thirds
242
Chromatic
243
C Major
X Scale
Y Chords
244
Thirds
245
Chromatic
246
Gb Major
X Scale
Y Chords
247
Thirds
248
Chromatic
249
G Major
X Scale
Y Chords
250
Thirds
251
Chromatic
252
High Gb
High Ab
High A
Flute